The Folly Of Ego

collected poetry and prose of
David Edward Wagner

DWM

Certain poems have appeared previously
in the following publications:

Linus Cain: a dark fable
Meditating With An Erection
The Last Innocent Man Has Died
A Passing Glance
The Huckabuck volumes 1-3
Short Fuse: volumes 79-82

Published in the United States of America by
David Wagner Media
DWM
davidedwardwagner@gmail.com

Other books by David Edward Wagner

Linus Cain: a dark fable
Marvelous Things
Anchors No More
Swill

Dedication

This collection of poetry is dedicated to Mongi Yacoubi, Don Brown, and Darioush Sami.

For lighting darkened paths, I thank you.

Introduction

Like the early pencil sketches of Picasso, the poems here are a map to David Wagner, the divining rods vibrating in the direction of what would be.

I met David in 1996, in the swamps of Georgia, when some of these poems were first coming into creation. He was a delicate artist soul, a Puck bursting with potency and the hard-to-capture urgency of youth. In that myopic haze, many dreams are uttered and many talents gestate, but it's only later that you can look back and see the map to success emerging.

Maybe it was his quirky humor and charm, maybe it was the quiet confidence of his art, but you knew David was *one of those.* So, it is with great pleasure that I write this introduction to the David I met in the woods. Rarely are we brave enough to let people into our process because it is messy, and yet that's what David has done here. Taking us back nearly 20 years, these poems allow us into the first hatched dreams, the horny, the soiled, the vulnerable, the lost, the clever, the sardonic, the shitty bellies, the chanting mantras, the voodoo nights, and the sometimes inflated, but always painfully authentic, longings of youth.

Together, we remember the defining moments when we looked around and chose to live.

- Nancy Stohlman, January 28, 2014

Nancy's latest book is "Going Short: an introduction to flash fiction".
Visit her at nancystohlman.com.

The Folly Of Ego
Collected poetry and prose of
David Edward Wagner

Your Eyes (1999)

Stand tall.
Let your
Self
Be your
Shield.
Never look back
There is
Nothing
Worse than that.
Stumble if you must
Crawl on
Knees and wings
But always
Continue forward.

Your eyes told me of your hidden pain
I hope you don't mind.
Don't worry though
We all have them.
Mine is here
On this page
Between these lines
On the
Other side
Of
This
Black ink.

So, Here's the Deal (1994)

It's like checkin' yourself
at 2 a.m.
on the side of the highway
somewhere in Kentucky
and thinkin' that the endless drone of speeding vehicles
sounds almost
like the endless drone of crashing waves
and your body feels too awkward to sleep
and you can see your breath
and you're glad
(if for nothing else)
at least you're
no longer
eighteen and kneeling in the pantry with the
broken glass
to your wrist
tiptoeing between dust particles.
Those were the days,
Weren't you afraid?
Nah, not you.
You were full of:

                    10% apathy
                    20% anger
                    30% boredom
                    15% disillusionment
                    15% stupidity
                    and 10% innocence.

Do You Know? (1995)

What will you do this time?
What exactly are you willing to do?
What are you able to do?
What is it that motivates ya?
What is it that drives you forward?
What is it that burns you?
      teases you?
      reminds you?

      A certain blend of
      candy
      and
      barbed wire
      leaves
      me
      curious if
      nothing
      else

Shoulder-blade-rip-chord.
See that ground
rising?

See that house there on the corner?
See through that window and gaze upon that sweet woman.
See into her eyes and tell her everything is going to be fine.

And then you hit hard.

Here We Are (1996)

Here we are.
> Inevitably confused
> Understandably concerned,
> Unquestionably combustible.

With time barking in our ears
and hope around every next corner
waiting for us like a forlorn lover beside the tomb
of a silent telephone.

The world is a lot like us, my love.
Struggling with existence amid a flurry of circumstance.

The Thought of You (1999)

Define greatness.
Is it a thing tangible?
Possessing mass?
Is it
the deed itself
or
the action inherent
in the deed?
Is it millions
or
just one,
curled up next to you,
toes tapping yours?

Intermission (a cold bed at 3 a.m.) (1996)

Sometimes, when you're lying in bed, too tired to masturbate, yet too distracted to sleep, your mind goes skipping down cobblestone paths of nostalgia and desire and devils and wishes, and you can't help but think they all mean the same thing, they all smell the same and taste the same and feel the same, and that they only just wear different masks. So, your mind makes a daisy chain for your soul with no other motive than to slip off its panties and plunge in, all innocence left scattered like leaves on life's front yard. Rake it up and throw it on the compost heap along with your ideals and your childhood and your family and your best guesses and your pain and your blindness. You open your eyes and face the darkness and all you get in return are tears and solitude and one unending vision of wrapping your warm and trembling lips around her soft, brown nipple and, as you do, it hardens, and upon further inspection, you see it is now a shotgun barrel and you smile and suck harder, waiting for the split-second of intensity before you join the others. But it never comes. No escape, not for you. Some of us are here for the duration. Some of us are here forever and the single thought that surges through your system is that you have loved and you have been loved. You repeat it out loud, "I have loved and I have been loved." You repeat your mantra and sleep finely comes, slowly and silently, and in the morning, you crawl out of bed, urinate, and continue to wait patiently for your turn.

Random Last Thought of Jesus Christ (1998)
(somewhere between "Are you serious?" and "Who said that?")

"Eloi, Eloi, lama sabachthani?"

I was backed against the wall like a thief, like a lingering stranger.
My heart beat fast and my feet nervously shuffled. I sucked in air
and spit it out as if it filled me with spores of mold and fungus.
Was it worth it? All of it?
I imagine her tongue, tasting of wine, caressing my own tongue.
Her smell, opium and jasmine. Arms, slender and sure, cradle me.
Dark hair spills down her shoulders and puddles on my chest. Our
bodies, damp with sin.
But in a moment of fear, I chose the other way.
My blood boils bitter in my heart.
Let them stone me.
Let them tear my eye from its socket,
My heart from my chest.
I will show them.
I won't die. I will live forever.
Stones shall strike like roses.
Curses shall ring as gospel.
Spittle sweeter than ale.
I will consume my own flesh and when none remains, float to
Heaven as spiritual foam.

They will never destroy me.
I am less than shadow, more than flesh.
I am the whisper you think you hear.
I am the nothingness in all things.

And
One day you will come to me.
I will not have to return.
You
will come to me.

San Francisco (Autumn) (1999)

Porno on Market Street
Egg rolls on Washington
Everything else on Haight
My knees are sore
A sure a sign as any that
I've not gotten younger this year.

Last night's rain
Creeps through my jeans
As
I
Lay here
On
Green grass
      Under
      Burning sun
      Among
      The grandeur of humanity
And write these simple words.

Silence (1999)

Silence
Is
A
Thing
To
Be
Best appreciated
From
Certain
Lips.

One, Two, Three… (1997)

Are the
wagons circled
and the women and children
stashed in a safe place?
Are your eyes and ears peeled
for any sign of movement?
Shall we
swoop
down
for the kill
with Wagner blaring
like harmonious thunder
or should we strike
without warning,
silent
like a
final breath?

Don't panic.
Keep calm.
Hold your
ground
and
wave your flag.

Don't fall
with a bullet
in your back.
Make the fuckers
shoot you
between
the eyes.

Hey God, Pick Up, Aisle Three (1998)

Elegant words
Are for the weak minded
And the
Weak hearted,
Trying
To make their shadow
Loom
High above
The
Monotonous passage of bodies
From
Here to there to the afterworld.
Pick me up,
Spread me out
Like
The first knifeful of jelly
On
Your favorite bread.
Bring me back.
Back to now.
Back to creation.
Back to the beauty.
Back to the harmony.
Back to myself.
Back to the point in time
When
Elbow room
Was not
Just a concept
And
I couldn't beg enough
For you
To crumple me into a ball
And put me out of the way.

Death is a Profession (2002)

Killing myself with kindness
         A drink of that
         A smoke of this
         Each day alive another shovelful of soil
            Plucked
            From my grave
            Six feet down and molding
            Collecting insects
            Turning to bone and dust

Death is a profession
with no remnants of respectability inherent
         A brilliant mind decayed
         A beautiful face withered
         Then leathered
         Then gone
         Only a skeletal smile remains
         Nothing left to be loved
         But
         A memory of what you were
         And,
         Tell me please,
         What were you?

Breakfast in Head (1996)

Awake.
Cast the sleep from your eyes
And gaze
Onto the beauty
Your
Thin eyelids
Shielded you from
All these years.

Pass into consciousness.
Dip your toe
In the
Pond of reality
And smile
Because it is
Almost bath water.

Take your first ambling steps
Out of bed
And come here
Here
Here
Bask in whatever glow you feel.
Beauty is yours to decide.

Awake
To the dawn of a new day.
Virgin starlight
Warms
My tired muscles
My pale flesh
My monkey
And
My sorrows.

Sit beside me,

I've
Already poured the coffee
And we'll swap stories
                spit
                     recipes
                          neurosis.
We'll
Share the
Last bit of bread,
Chewing slowly,
As
To
Not end it
Too
Soon.

The Man Who Was Alone (a fable) (1996)

He cried out that he was alone, that there was no understanding, that the world was too big and too calloused for one such as he. An artist. A dreamer. A quiet thinker. He struggled against the tide, he fell into many pits, he pushed aside those who were most like he, thinking they were too weak to see the struggle through, thinking them as only a hindrance to his own advance.

He began to walk one day and eventually was standing outside of a great city with buildings of gold and streets paved with jewels and the bones of the city's fallen so that none would forget those who had come before them.

He sat alone on a hill overlooking this fine place for two days, hardly eating or drinking, his mind drifting. Below, he could hear the pleasant sounds of a bazaar, he could smell savory meats cooking upon open fires, he could almost taste the wine upon the lips of beautiful women, but still, he dared not join the celebration. Why should I break this bond of contemplation I have established for a few moments of fleeting pleasure, he thought. Will I not miss the soft company of some fair woman even more tomorrow if I allow myself the dignity of knowing her now? Will my tongue not ache for one more sweet morsel of lamb or duck tomorrow if I allow myself to consume such delicacies tonight? Will my heart and mind not grow pained and cry when they find no soul to share my deepest hopes and fears with? It is better to not know such things, for the loss of them only slaps your face like a lover with wounded pride.

On the third day, a pair of children, a boy and a girl, came upon the man as they made their way over the hill towards a tiny village in the Great Woods, to trade cloth and meat for berries and herbs. They invited the man to go and join the revelry below, for it was the final day of the bazaar and it would not be back for several months. The man declined, telling them that they were not ready for one such as he, an individual soul in this land of emptiness. He was too strong, he said, to join in their mindless distraction and excess. Thank you, but no, he would do just fine to sit here on the hill, counting the buildings and trees by day and the stars and the lights of the fires by night.

"Suit yourself," said the young girl with eyes of ice and hair of raven-blue, "the sky shall not fall today. The blood in your veins is thickening, it is turning to clay. Will you not stand? Will you not dance one step to the tune leaking from your mother's womb? Will you not put one hand in yours? Will you not appease just one stranger who might love you? You may or may not be a wicked man, you may or may not be a just and wise man, you may or may not be here when we return in three days time, but the corn will die either way, the sky might always be blue, and nothing shall come of such suffering."

The children left a loaf of bread and a fistful of meat with the man and continued on their way. At first, the man was angry, then sad, then confused. He took the loaf of bread and flung it at the sky. He took the fistful of meat and hurled it at the ground. He pulled a single strand of hair from his head and with it wove a cloak of great intricacy and began to walk again. He walked away from the city, away from companionship, away from all things painful.

Except each morning, when he awoke, it was still there.

Truth Be Told… (2001)

I fail to find the romance in this anymore,
This grand, empty shit.

Untitled Poem Written Late One Evening (1997)

What
Are those rustling footsteps
Outside
My door?
Is it a wolf?
Or a deer?
Or maybe the three-headed hell hound
Coming to tell me
Timmy's in trouble
He fell down the well
And
Is
Dangling by only a thin and brittle root.
It
Could possibly be
You
Coming back to kiss me goodnight
But
It's more likely
A hungry opossum
Or
The grim reaper
Or
A skunk.

The Brittle Walk (1996)

The
Brittle walk
Eggshell souls
Over
Paper maché
Trail
Bite the bullet
And
Count off the strokes
One
Two
Three…

Intermission (New Orleans) (1996)

And then there's those times when you're lonely and horny and walking through the streets of New Orleans by yourself and the freshly fallen rain reflects the street lamps and your own crazed face, and it puts a slight chill in your body that makes you feel just a bit more like a dying breed, and the only comfort you know you'll receive tonight is your head laying on your backpack somewhere in some dark alley while your bones rattle like Gene Krupa gone mad and your mind, wandering to more important things like the honey-vinegar of freedom and staying alive till the morning light, only partially registers the traffic and the big, burly man in black hawking in front of the strip joint around the corner. "Hey man, we got some beautiful girls." "No thanks, man." "What's a matter? You don't like girls? We got the finest women in this city. Black girls. Blonde girls. We got two chicks who'll eat each other out, and let me tell ya, it's something." "Nah, thanks anyway." "Your loss." "I'm sure."

And over the night, your mind does wander back to those girls. So incredibly beautiful, so ready and able to trade flesh and illusion, to give those who want what they want, making five hundred dollars a night on a stage in front of fifty strangers, caressed in a pinkish glow with AC/DC blaring in the background. Do they know, do they care, if there is more to life than spreading those long legs, more to life than plastic breasts and shiny new sports cars, more to life than the table full of married business executives, in town without their wives, pumping out fifty bucks a pop to get dragged off into some back room so some nice smelling, lovely young lady can grind up and down on their stiff penis. "Just relax, baby, I'll take care of you. You can touch me anywhere but between the legs, okay?" "Okay."

And you want to take her by the hand and lead her out of that place, past the mirrored ceilings and the groping eyes, out into the street and say, look around, past the dirt and decay, and the see the beauty and magic, feel it on your skin. You want to drag her into the countryside and say, look around, past the illusion of all you see, and taste the air, feel this harmony. You want to drag her up the mountain, to the very peak, and say, look around, past the veil of humanity and see the blueprint of creation, the majesty and humility. You want to drag her to the foot of God's throne and say nothing, both of you content to simply sit and wait for the second act to begin.

Ramblings of the Mind at 10:22 (1997)

Love.
Love!
Love! Love!! Love!!!
LOVE
love

What is love?
Love
Love
Love
I think I'd rather
Have
A paper cut.

On Letting These Things Go (2002)

All prices are inevitable and relative.
You know that
better than most I would
even venture to say.
> But still you press onward,
> pre-occupied with equal thoughts of love and death,
> of that which never goes and that which
> you must leave behind,
> of what is yours and what is Ours.

> This does not belong to you.
> This does not belong to you.
> This does not belong to you.
> Nor to me.
> It is not mine to give or to share.
> Only to
> release
> to the whims of fortune and fate.

You've only one chance to love something properly
then it moves on,
as do you,
and if you are lucky or unafraid,
patient or true,
you may eventually learn to love that something
in that proper way
and
realize it never really did move on,
and neither did you,
you both simply grew into the love that always seemed
too big
to handle
all alone.

Untitled Poem (the quiet Moroccan…) (2002)

The quiet Moroccan told me
    "Death is around every corner"
    and
    I couldn't help but agree.

Thoughts like this guide my every move.

The Folly of Ego (2002)

The song ends
      Try not to linger on past melodies
Another one is soon to begin.

      Ask not for more truth
      There is no room for
      More than one.

The answer came quickly
So I searched for my pen
Desiring to make it tangible
And by the time black ink
      Touched paper
          It was gone.

This is the folly of ego.

The Symptoms are the Cure (1998)

Saul Brimbraker generally liked to sleep until around ten in the morning, most often waking up at nine forty-two. Sometimes he stirred as late as ten-thirteen and sometimes as early as nine twenty-three, but nine forty-two seemed to be the average. Of course, that was Mountain Standard Time and under the currently accepted Greenwich standard for temporal qualification.

This was a morning, however, that began with Saul not only waking up at nine forty-two on the dot, but also feeling slightly queasy. A quick self-diagnosis found that the problem was not diverticulosis as he first feared (Saul carried a deep-seated belief that one day, for his sins, he would develop this disease that he knew nothing about and thus feared unsubstantially), but instead was simply in his stomach. He had what his mother would have called a 'shitty belly.'

"Does my baby have a shitty belly?" or "Not now, momma's got a shitty belly."

Being a slow to wake, Saul stumbled, using only momentum and blind familiarity, to the bathroom. A flick of the switch brought a light to the room and Saul yawned in unison with his tummy growling, although slightly off key.

It could have been the pizza. It could have been the chicken wings that had been hot enough to make his eyes and nose drip. It could have been the company the night before, the droning conversation, the time of year, the influx of information, the color of his pajamas, the whiffle ball bat he owned as a child, the price of warmth, the delays, the doubts, the 'Banana Boat Song,' or even the Spaniards.

He looked at himself. His reflection made him lonely.

He decided it was the chicken wings and wiped a dot of toothpaste off of the reflection of his eye.

Tonight, I am the Silent Storm (1999)

Tonight, I am the silent storm.
Tonight, I am strangely calm.
Tonight, I am waiting.
Tonight, I am a fury of thought.
Tonight, I am hurting.
Tonight, I am alone.
Tonight, I have no shoulder to reach for.
Tonight, I want to disappear.
Tonight, I long for warmth.
Tonight, I can touch no one.
Tonight, emotions fight for position.
Tonight, I am the top of the food chain.
Tonight, I am dynamic in my own particular way.
Tonight, I will not be released.
Tonight, I want to claw my mind from my skull and burn it, bleach
it, boil it, sterilize it, purify it, re-wire it, destroy it, at least trade it in
for a more reliable model.
Tonight, this is all I have.

Art is... (2000)

Art is light wrapped in shadows
Art is shadow blinded by light
Art is beauty in the guise of horror
Art is horror masquerading as beauty
Art is sadness imitating joy
Art is joy overcome with shadow
Art is a home, a safe harbor, a way out
Art is a trap, a stormy sea, a moonless night
Art is all I have
Its fire keeps me warm though it threatens to consume me
Its charm keeps me happy, though its promiscuity continuously
breaks my heart
But you think you can keep it satisfied
        By writing one more sentence
        One more word
        Dropping one more tear
        Mixing blood and semen with black ink
        But a creature of such beauty is never
        Sedate or humble
        It always needs more

That is Where You Find Your Weakness (2000)

Random thoughts
Words on paper
Make it fit
Make it rhyme
Make it Grand and Important
Waste no time
Never look up
Do not burn precious seconds
Crystalline instances
By looking away from the tip of your pen making concrete these thoughts swirling around your head, all battling for release, you need to maintain focus to keep in control of them all, they are easily handled alone, but when they pile up and grow agitated and begin buzzing and nipping you must be cautious and steady, you must maintain a sense of calm and an air of authority about you, remember, those single and multi-syllabic bastards can smell fear and when they do, they become blood-crazed and will not rest until they are fed, until they are appeased.
So,
Just a reminder,
Do not look away from these words,
From the whiteness around them,
And do not,
Above all else,
Look into her eyes.
That is where you find your weakness.
That is where your weakness
Devours you.

Intermission (New Orleans #2) (1996)

"You can stay at my place, and I'll get you high if you suck my dick."
"No thanks. I'm okay."
"New Orleans is a rough place, bro. I'll take care of you."
"That's cool, man, I'm taken care of."
"C'mon, brother. How about I suck you first?"
"No thanks, man, that ain't my scene."
"Alright then. You get cold, you know where to find me."
"Yeah, see ya."

And the rest of the night progresses.
A few beers.
A couple of jazz bands, blues bands, rock bands.
The hustlers wanting your money, your lips, your blood, your soul.
The pack on your back is getting heavier by the block.
Up and down those streets you go, kept on your feet by the rain and the fear and the knowledge that around that next corner you may be saved, you may be beaten, you may be left for dead, but it doesn't matter.
Esplanade. Bourbon. Decatur. Burgundy. Past the gay clubs and the strip joints and the all-night bars. It smells like a wet sweater left in a plastic bag for far too long. You can actually taste the city on your tongue, did you know that? You can open your mouth and the city makes it start to water. It tastes of sin and of magic and of power and of things that you are not able to comprehend, so you settle for acceptance, as you curl up in a door stoop, your head in the shadows, your feet getting wet.

World Opens Up (1999)

World opens up
Smiles
Drift away.
You
       Wash your hands
                Come in for dinner

Don't stay out too late.
There are
Demons with prying eyes everywhere.
                Waiting.
                Salivating.

Don't panic.
Close your eyes.
Hope for the best.

2:16 PM and Holding (Chicago) (2001)

And here we sit.
The burn-outs
The businessmen
The hustlers
The wanderers
All passing by
Looking at one another
Until
It comes close to
Eye contact
Then
Look away,
Nobody
Wants to see
Behind
The other's gaze.

Look at all
The beautiful girls
Neatly dressed and
Smelling of roses.

Look at all
The handsome men
Groomed and
Well-pressed.

I think
The woman
Next to me
Is
Dying.
Slumped
Ragged
Gone fetal
On the

Corner of
State and Adams.
I think
It would be best
For her to
Leave this place
To drop over
Dead
Right here on
The street.
But
Before she went,
She should stand up
And face them all
Howl in their ears
Assault their existence.
"Fuck You,"
She should scream,
"Burn in Hell
"Monsters
"Blind walkers
"Shuffling zombies.
"I hope this city
"Falls down on all of you!"
There are ninety shades of shadow
In my sight
And it seems appropriate.
There is an
Ungodly hum
A stale stench
A measured indifference.

The sky
Looks like rain
I think
I'll go.

Paradise (2002)

It is only when you leave paradise
That you can
Appreciate
Its grandeur, its appeal.
It would be nice to
Sleep today
To linger in the sun
And
Remain unbothered
And unburdened by the trials of the day.

What it all comes down to,
I guess,
Is not asking for too much
And
Understanding what it takes to accomplish anything
Especially
Amid the
        Unpredictability
            Of the world these days.

Plus Tax (1997)

Tell me the price.
Is it a hundred dollars?
A thousand?
A million?
Is it my soul
Or
My sanity?
Is it my favorite childhood memory?
Is it an arm
Or
Possibly a leg?
Could it be my future?
My furniture?
My clothes?
My dreams?
Is it my eyes, ears, or tongue?
Tell me the price.
I'll give anything to hold you right now.

Time to Disintegrate (2001)

I cannot wait until I am an old man.
A bit more content.
Less easily distracted, more focused.
Able to devote more of my time to writing, to thinking, to reading,
to making music, and less time lusting after women, exotic locales,
self-destruction, and dream chasing.
My skin thin and dry, my back bent and stiff, my penis shriveled
and dead, but my mind, my spirit, fresh, pulsing, alive.
And then I'll gulp in that last breath, try for another, think better of
it, and simply exhale, mid-way through a sentence, the end of a
thought, now it is only time to disintegrate.

The Dawn of Such Predictability (2002)

The dawn of such predictability is
That which comes on unobtrusively
That which is welcomed in with a nod of the head
Or a breaking of loaves.
Don't fear the knife in your back
      The spear through your chest
      The burning in your ear is
      Just a voice from your past
      Telling you
      To tuck your shirt in and don't slouch.
      Can't you see the slobbering masses gawking?
      The celebrated few echoing within their
      own ashen minds.
      There is a feeling I get sometimes
      Which
      Leaves me alone on some hillside
      Overlooking lazy ripples on a fragile pond
      Writing words to help me understand
      Such feelings
      Such hillsides
      Such lazy ripples upon fragile ponds.
      And it is somewhere in the midst of
      Such melancholy musings
      That a certain face,
      A certain word or melody,
      Carries me to a far kinder place
      Than these
      Rows of humanity.

           This is my cradle and my grave.
           A brown lizard on an old oak tree
           The only silent witness
           To both my birth and demise.

Watch Your Feet, You Almost Stepped in Love (1997)

I accidentally
Stumbled into your eyes
While
Walking down the street
Minding my own business
Thinking of unfortunate things
Like
The suicide rate of artists
And
My own place in the world.
You brushed your hair
Off of your face
Off of your neck
And
We smiled at one another
And
It could be possible
That
I let my gaze
Linger
A moment too long
Because
The slope of your neck
From ear to shoulder
Stayed in my mind for days afterwards
And I
Felt the noose
Tighten
Around the throat
Of my heart
And
The knuckles
Whiten
In a death grip

And I wished,
If only for a moment,
I
Could
Translate the universe
Into
Simple words
Like
Love
Compassion
Trust
And
Hello.

Fireside Chat with Nobody (2001)

These quiet times are what get me through.
Listening to music from behind a curtain.
Watching smoke curl and fade,
Shadows stretch, life blossoms effortlessly, continuously.
Feeling myself grow peaceful and settled.
Believing in nothing and everything.
Trusting in the unfolding of events beyond control.
Knowing love evolves but never fades.
Writing words that mean nothing.

We are the Best (1996)

I see myself
In the thin skin
That tears so easily
And
The dried snot and food
On withered faces.
I see myself
In the sunken yellow eyes,
Dulled
In sullen defeated stares
And
In hands wrinkled and rigid
And in gnarled finger and toe nails
And in twisted, bruised bodies
And in tears for someone to hold
And in the beds where dignity fades
like fog in the rising sun,
And in every lingering look
And
Cherished moment.
I see myself
And
Then
Quickly turn away.
I've
Never
Been
One
For
Mirrors.

A Prayer to Myself (1994)

That what does not
Kill me
Only serves to annoy me.
I want to leave my flesh
(I want to leave my flesh)
I want to be born into light
I want to be born into energy

That what does not
Kill me
Only serves to excite me.
Let the executioner
Rub my skin
With oil
And
Let the corpse of the shadow of the memory
Of the last proud man
Walk beside me and tell me
Of mercy
And of justification.

That what does not
Kill me
Only serves to comfort me.
Like a mother.
Like a strong drink
Or
A long walk.
Now
Is the time
I pray for numbness.
Now
Is the time
I pray for fresh air.
Now
Is the time

I pray for the other thought.

That what does not
Kill me
Only forces me to continue living
And so I shall
With as much
Grace and courage
As one can muster
When
Clumsy and afraid.

A Poem for my Mother (1994)

All I did was
Scream
Until my voice was
Raw
And my throat
Bloody.

I screamed for help.
I cried for mercy.
I begged for forgiveness.
I prayed for answers.
I heard no reply,
Simply
Wind through trees.

All I did was
Walk
Until my steps were weak
And my feet
Bloody.

I searched for peace.
I called for home.
I remembered my companion.
I prayed for answers.
I found nothing,
Simply
Sunlight on my face.

All I did was
Fight
The world
Until my back was
Bent
And my hands
Bloody.

I drove back the sun.
I harnessed the wind.
I built great temples.
I prayed for answers.
I now have nothing left,
Simply
Memories of it all.

I felt pity for my plight.
I cursed God.
I wept for the living
As much as the dead.
I found refuge in a
Hole.
Apart from
Mind and
Soul and
Heart.

And,
Just when I thought I had
Nothing,
I heard the wind through the trees
And
Felt the sun on my face
And
Remembered the times together
And
I
Found the strength to
Start
Again.

Acid in the Punchbowl (1998)

What
  Is
    That
      In
        The
          Carpet?

Is it the river of tears
Or
Is
It
Just
Millions and millions
Of
Semi-glossy partially translucent ants
Swarming towards me
Swarming around me
Swarming on me?
But
Why are you smiling at me
With
That
Blank look
On
Your face?
Why is she withdrawn in the corner
Sucking her thumb
Asking for
      "Mommy
      come make it all go away.
      Please make the monsters go away.
      You must
      Help me
      For I cannot dispel these
      Beasts
      All by myself.

I
Think I need some comfort
Some reassurance
A strong drink.
Something.
I'm not strong enough,
I see that now.
          I see that now.
                    I see that now…"

There is my friend
Tickling himself
Laughing like
A nun on ether

     Two old men
     Sit
     Proudly upon the couch
     Their tongues lapping at one another
     Waves on unexplored shores.

          Susan is screaming of bison.

          I think Paul has urinated on himself.

I know it's true
I know its true
I know it's true
What is true
Is it true
What is truth
If you break it down
And down
And
Down
And
     Down
          And

                Down
You'll see that it all comes back to
One
Thing
One impulse
One stimulus
One heartbeat

                I see now
                I see now

                        The dogs bite.
                        They nip my heels.

Who made this punch?
Sarah, who made this
Yum yum yummy punch?

        Can't anybody see me?
        My god.
        I'm Invisible
        I'm Sterile.

                Love flairs its fleshy wings
                And
                Turns two heads
                Then three
                And by the end
                There is flesh
                And spit
                And fire
                And hot wax
                And growling…

Two guys walk into a bar   what is this
One of 'em shoulda ducked   what's going on
Hahahahahahahahha   what do you want
Do you get it   from me
That's so fucking funny
One of them woulda ducked   take your

Oh shit, that's fucking funny

A man in the corner
Slowly constructs a
Crucifix out of
Average household items

With a far away
Empty (yet hopeful)
Look on his face
He
Turns on the television

I need to hear some
Blue Oyster Cult
Is there any
Blue Oyster Cult
In this fucking house?
Hey man
You got any BOC
I need to hear "Don't fear the Reaper"
Right now
Or I'm gonna
Fucking freak!

pinching eyes
off of me
you godless stains!

two girls
embrace and cry
they
are in so much
mental agony
so empty
so beautiful
so lost
innocent in
their realizations

Wow
I feel so tuned in, man
My excrement is the universe
smell me
taste me

Is that mango punch?
Do I taste mango?
(The smacking of lips)
Mango?

What

does it all mean?
It all comes back to love.

It all comes back to pain.

What does it all mean?
Everything is connected.
Everything is chaos.

He giggles and hiccups.

          What does it all mean?
          Everything is hand clapping
          In joy.
          Everything is god turning
          The knives
          In our backs.

She shrieks in terror

          What does it all mean?
          Everything is a circle.
          Everything is a smear.

A conga line forms.

          What does is all mean?
          I'm a part of the whole.
          I'm apart and in a hole.

    One
    Man
    Sits
    On
    The
    Counter
    Silent
    And still

A muffled shout and the power goes out.

Conversation with a Faded Love (1998)

"Where are you going?"
"I'm walking away."
"Why?"
"What do you mean why? You know why. This is futile. Useless.
We're spinning in circles, for Christ's sake."
"What do you mean by that?"
"Jesus, are you blind? We spend more time worrying about
everything but what is really important to us. We forgot why we are
here. Why we fell in love. When I see you, it might as well be a
stranger."
"Don't say that."
"Why not, it's true. Isn't this supposed to be about truth?"
"Yes, but…"
"No buts, not anymore. I'm leaving and that's that."
"But I love you."
"I know."
"I gave you my heart and my soul."
"You gave it freely. I never asked for it."
"That's supposed to make it better? You never asked for it?
Bullshit."
"I'm sorry."
"I'm sure."
"It makes more sense this way."
"Whatever."

> A deep breath.
> Pleading eyes.
> Both wishing it could be better.
> No words left to say.
> Time to heal.
> Letting go is a nightmare.

Episodes of Jubilation (1999)

Episodes
Of jubilation.

Answers
Swarming

Glacier
Spasm
Leaves
      2 dead
      13 injured
          and
          an
          irreparable
          fissure
          in the
          structure.

Who
Knows
Why
Some fires die.
It is the
Way of nature
I suppose.

A hand
  Can only
    Grasp
      So much
        Before the
            Fingers ache
              And
                Bend
                  And
                    Clutch in

Malformed
Claws.

The Jaundiced eye of
Nostalgia
Has loosened my strings
And
Exclaiming,
  "Lies and shadows
  Only
  Grow longer
  As the
  Sun sets,"
I leap to my feet
And
When I land
Sit down again as if
Nothing happened.

  And time doesn't take away
  It only gives
  And good luck
  Is at least as valuable
  As good timing.

There is no shame
In
Following those
Bread crumbs, Sweetie,

  They were left there
  For you.

Intermission (Santa Barbara) (1997)

Sitting here, passing this time, killing this day, this hour, this year, this life. Thinking of things important and not so important, watching the people walk by, the beautiful, the ravaged, the old and young, all taking one more step towards inevitability, each breath sucked in and out of their moist lungs carry them ever closer to the dust of creation. For some I feel sorry, watching beauty fade, talent wasted, truth passed aside. For most I feel either pity or nothing, too many impersonal beings to care about them all. They are the nameless ones, the mass average, the pulsing multitudes that hold back, wear down, destroy, the things in life that are special or unique. They are the ones who are bound by their lack of effort, their inability to imagine or dare. I try to feel nothing for them. I attempt at least an honest indifference, but can only truly feel anger, can only truly find resentment. And it is against such a dull, lifeless background that some stand out, glowing with an almost surreal brilliance and clarity, and it is to those people I cling, knuckles white and shaking, as the weight of the world tries to pull us down. But we are stronger than it knows. Yes, we are. You need only look into my eyes, I will tell you everything. Here, pull up a chair and pour yourself a drink, the night is still in the distance and we've nothing to do but die. Let us enjoy a few moments. Let us marvel in such company and conversation for they are sure not to come again.

The Last Innocent Man Has Died (1999)

The last innocent man has died
With
His cock in his hand and his tail planted firmly between his legs.

The last innocent man has died
In
A feeding frenzy, in a fishbowl, in a stadium of ignorance.

The last innocent man has died
And
The mourners painted lovely portraits of discarded dreams.

The last innocent man has died
And
The world moved on,
A bit wiser,
A bit sadder,
A bit reluctant,
But
It moved on
Nonetheless.

I Cannot Deny These Feelings… (2000)

I cannot deny these feelings
Nor can I pursue them.
Once again,
The universe sarcastically provides what I ask for.

Lullaby (1995)

Outside kneeling
Begging
Stealing
Feeling just a little bit impure

I thought it was a Sunday
A Thursday or
A Monday
But I didn't really know for sure

There was a part of me a yellin'
A peekin'
And a tellin'
A spellin' out the poems in the stars

And this is what I'm sayin'
I'm writin'
And I'm playin'
Never let them make you who you are.

About the Author

From Ohio, David Edward Wagner now splits his time between Berkeley, California and Istanbul, Turkey.

He has an MA in philosophy, a lovely wife, and a beautiful son.